STRETCHING YOUR LIMITS

Step-by-Step

Instructions for over 30

Stretch Band Stretches

14 PEAKS

DEDICATION

This book is dedicated to all who are in pursuit of excellence. May you push your limits, embrace the challenge, and stretch your way... to the top.

ACKNOWLEDGMENTS

I would like to thank Faye Viviana for her help in professionally composing the exercises in this book and for the instructional photos, as well.

TABLE OF CONTENTS

Chapter 1
Stretching: The Long and the Short of It

So, you're ready to stretch yourself to the top. That is awesome! You probably know what the word stretch means, but do you *really* know what it means? Don't worry, we'll explain exactly what it entails.

The true definition is often misunderstood and the fact is there are several definitions which further complicate the matter. When it comes to stretching in terms of fitness and physical health:

> *Stretching is the process of positioning specific parts of the body into a placement that will lengthen or elongate the muscles as well as the soft tissues in the area.*

Whew, that is a mouthful.

The main types of stretching in dance, gymnastics, and athletics are static and dynamic.

STATIC STRETCHES

Static stretching exercises are ones that involve no movement. They take place from a stretched position. The pose is held for a certain amount of time and in a specific way.

DYNAMIC STRETCHES

Dynamic stretching exercises are done with movement such as jumping, swinging, and skipping. These are the exercises you want to do first because they get your blood flowing and your body ready for the big stuff.

Jumping jacks are a good example of dynamic stretches. You are stretching your body, but adding movement to the action. There is a chapter reserved for both static stretches and dynamic stretches, so if you're confused about the difference, hang in there. You'll master them both soon.

ACTIVE AND PASSIVE STRETCHING

To add more to the mix, there are also active and passive stretching exercises. Although every stretch is either static or dynamic, and those are either active or passive, there are further variations like MET (Muscle Energy Techniques), ballistic stretching, and PNF (Proprioceptive Neuromuscular Facilitation), stretching to name a few.

We'll get into some dynamic stretching exercises and will also focus on static stretches that fall into the passive category.

These are done with a ballet stretch band which is a type of resistance band specially designed for those who are stretching for classic ballet, contemporary dance, gymnastics, martial arts, or athletics.

THE BENEFITS OF STRETCHING

What's the big deal about stretching?

Stretching is important for a number of reasons. If it wasn't, we'd probably all skip it for the most part and get right to the fun part like a good, hard workout, performance, or competition. That wouldn't be smart at all. Here's why.

What is the first thing a baby, or even a dog, does when he or she wakes up? They stretch. That's because it is such an important action and it comes almost instinctively.

WHAT DOES STRETCHING DO?

- ## IMPROVES FLEXIBILITY

Stretching improves flexibility which can certainly boost your performance when it comes to ballet, dance, and/or gymnastics.

- ## REDUCES RISK OF INJURY

Stretching helps your risk of injury because it enables your joints to work at their full range of motion and also allows your muscles to work at their maximum capacity.

- ## INCREASES BLOOD FLOW

Blood flow is increased in the muscles and soft tissues in the area you are stretching. That's not all…

There are some additional benefits of stretching. It's a fact stretching can help reduce pain. It also increases energy, enhances posture, and improves coordination. To top it off, stretching, like exercise, simply makes you feel better all the way around.

STRETCHING AND BALLET

Ballet is said to be the foundation of all forms of dance. It is also the most physically demanding and the most disciplined, as well.

Most agree ballet is an art, not a sport. It is a display of creative expression that is breathtaking to watch. It is extremely difficult to do.

There are favored physiques adopted in ballet, although some of these concepts are changing.

Typically, the average height of a female ballerina is about five foot three inches to five foot eight inches and they weigh between 85 to 130 pounds.

Male dancers are generally around five foot eight inches to six foot two inches tall and weigh about 135 to 165 pounds. Whether a male or female, ballet requires a relatively small person to be very, very strong.

A dancer must have super strong quadriceps, hamstrings, hips, gluteal, calf, feet, back, and core muscles. They must also have plenty of upper body strength.

When it comes to ballet, stretching is extremely important. In 2014, the Centers for Disease Control (CDC) required stretch and flexibility training to be implemented before each and every classical ballet technique class. There were far too many ballerinas ending up with serious injuries

The CDC said although such suggestions had been issued before, they had largely gone ignored. Ballet training requires the most stable, balanced, and integrated relationship between the spine and the extremities, it explained.

The organization went on to say the lack of proper stretch and flexibility training was resulting in injuries and postural alignment deformities which could last a lifetime. That is how important stretching is when it comes to ballet.

STRETCHING AND GYMNASTICS

Khabir Uddin Mughal, who is a writer for *Sportelogy Magazine* (http://sporteology.com/author/khabir-uddin-mughal/) believes gymnastics is the most difficult sport.

If you've ever participated in gymnastics, you may agree. There's nothing easy about turning your body into a living pretzel.

Gymnastics, like ballet, is beautiful to watch, but can be extremely difficult to perform. It's certainly not a sport for the faint of heart.

Typically, a gymnast must possess nine times his or her body weight in strength. When running the twenty-five meters to the vault, women reach sixteen or more miles per hour and men over twenty.

A gymnast must be able to tumble and vault up to thirteen feet for women and sixteen feet for men. In addition, the ability to balance, rotate, and spiral are a must.

A gymnast concentrates on the upper torso, core muscles, hip muscles, leg muscles, and arm muscles. It takes each of those areas being in tip-top shape to do what a gymnast does.

In order to achieve such a tall feat, you can imagine the hours of strenuous exercise required, not to mention the strain placed on the body during performances and meets. To help ensure injuries are avoided and performance is at its peak, both training and stretching are a must do.

STRETCHING FOR OTHER ATHLETES

Most sports and other physical activities benefit from stretching. Football, baseball, soccer, snow and water skiing, diving, swimming, and even horseback riding are best done after dynamic stretching.

Building flexibility through stretch bands is a great way to build strength, ensuring your muscles and soft tissues are well prepared for a good workout and a stellar performance, as well.

THE ART OF STRETCHING

Mobility is the ability to get around freely and with ease. It is everything to a performer of the arts, as well as to those in sports.

Flexibility is being able to bend without breaking. Mobility and flexibility go hand-in-hand. One helps the other.

Neither comes without a price, though. You have to work at it to be mobile and flexible enough to perform or compete.

Stretching improperly can do as much damage as not stretching at all, while proper stretching can bring a ton of positive results.

Concentrating on the area you are stretching is very important. Think about it. Visualize it. Become one with the body and you will reach new heights.

When you do stretching techniques the right way, you are going to improve your game. It's a given. It will make you more efficient, powerful, and you will have sustained endurance.

Stretching helps prevent injuries and can even help repair them, too. When done with skill and passion, you will be amazed what stretching can do for you. Stretching can help take you to the top.

Chapter 2
Static Stretching: The Art of Letting Go

Static stretching exercises are done by holding a particular stretch with no bouncing. These type of stretches help you become more flexible.

WHAT DO STATIC STRETCHING EXERCISES DO FOR YOU?

- **MAKES YOU MORE FLEXIBLE**

Static stretching actually makes your tension receptors less sensitive, so your muscles are able to relax, which in turn allows them to be stretched to a longer length.

- **RELEASES STRESS AND TENSION WITHIN THE MUSCLES**

Static stretches are really effective for relieving your muscles of the stress and tension that builds up during a dance class, performance, gymnastic routine, or workout. Your muscles tend to be warm after strenuous activity, making it easier to stretch.

FOCUS MATTERS

Static stretches focus on range of motion and flexibility. They are done nice and easy. It's a good idea to breathe deeply to allow oxygen to flow to the muscles, which is more important than you may think.

It all begins with a thing called cellular respiration which is the process your muscles use when they generate Adenosine triphosphate (ATP). ATP is a high-energy molecule that supplies your body with energy. It is your body's fuel. ATP molecules can be thought of as batteries for your body.

Your body gets oxygen when you breathe air. Then, it travels through the bloodstream where some of it goes immediately to your muscles to be used right away. Some, however, is stored by myoglobin which is a compound within your body which uses oxygen to break down glucose (blood sugar).

Glucose is used to create fuel for your muscles, called ATP. That is the reason it's important to breathe deeply when you are doing your stretches. It fuels your muscles.

Holding your stretches for ten to sixty seconds is optimal. There are many philosophies and opinions on exactly how long to hold them. Some say ten seconds done six times is best. Others say thirty seconds held two times is best. It is up to you.

As to how far you stretch, the perfect holding length is dependent on several other factors, like viscoelasticity. Viscoelasticity is the property of an object that has both viscous (resistant) and elastic qualities. It stretches, but with limits.

Take a rubber band, for instance. It stretches, but in order for it to remain a rubber band, there is a limit to how far it can stretch without breaking.

The same is true for our muscles. The measure of the viscoelasticity of your muscles is a key factor in determining how long you should hold a stretch. It's best to start out gently and not stress the muscles.

HOW FAR SHOULD I STRETCH?

Depends on…
- Your age (children and seniors should be especially careful)
- How tired your muscles are
- Presence of scar tissue
- Temperature of your muscles
- If you are dehydrated
- Your activity before the stretch
- Collagen and elastin content of your body (natural substances that help the body stretch and go back into place)
- Medical conditions (Diabetes, smoking, and connective tissue conditions)

WHAT IS A GREAT STRETCH?

Static stretching at its best is when you can feel your muscles stretch, but there is no pain. "No pain, no gain," does not apply when doing static stretches.

If you feel pain, you have pushed too far and run the risk of injuring your muscles, and then what?

You'll be sitting out dance classes, unable to make a gymnastics meet, or hanging out on the sidelines while the rest of the cheerleaders lead your team on. It can't be stressed enough to let your muscles do their thing without stretching them too hard or for too long.

STATIC STRETCHES

- Holding the middle or side splits
- Touching your toes and holding
- Lying on your back, pulling leg to chest and holding
- Sitting on the floor, leaning forward to touch the floor and then holding

Static stretching isn't meant to be hard or to hurt. Rather, it is a very important way of letting your body come back together properly after a hard workout or performance and to increase your flexibility.

Chapter 3
Dynamic Stretching

Although you might be tempted to go straight to your workout, recital, or competition, to be at your best and lower your risk of getting injured, you will need to take some time to warm up. That's where dynamic stretching exercises come in.

Dynamic stretching exercises are all about warming your muscles. They get your blood flowing and loosen muscles, ligaments, and joints.

Remember what happens when your blood brings oxygen to your muscles? They get all fired up.

You might think of dynamic stretching as fueling your car up so it's ready to rumble. *You're* ready to tumble.

WHAT DYNAMIC STRETCHING DOES

- Improves your range of motion
- Gets your blood flowing and your heart pumping
- Warms up your muscles, ligaments, and joints
- Brings oxygen to your muscles
- Stimulates your nervous system
- Prepares your body for more strenuous movements
- Keeps body in motion for full warm up through flowing movement
- Helps prevent injuries

EXAMPLES OF DYNAMIC STRETCHES

- Jumping jacks
- Arm and shoulder rolls
- Rolling your hips
- Rolling your neck
- Leg swings
- Jumping in place
- Side bends with continuous movement

ABOUT DYNAMIC STRETCHING

Dynamic stretching is active stretching, while static stretching is passive. Dynamic stretch exercises are done with motion, while static stretching exercises are not.

One important thing to remember while doing dynamic stretching is to avoid ballistic stretching. Ballistic is anytime you bounce during a stretch. This can cause injury, tearing the muscles. Dynamic stretches are movements done strategically and with control. They are generally done with gradual increases in speed and reach. Dynamic stretches gently warm you up.

In doing dynamic stretching, remember not to push your body. Even though the movements are controlled, you can still put too much stress on your muscles, joints, and ligaments, which defeats the purpose.

STRETCHES FOR DANCERS

The best type of dynamic stretches for you will depend, in part, on what you are doing after the stretching.

If you are a dancer, you will want to start with some dynamic stretches to get your heart warmed up, because dancing requires a lo of cardiovascular activity. The same is true with cheerleading and gymnastics.

Concentrate on the muscles, stances, and actions required while dancing or whatever art or sport you are performing. Those are the areas you want to be sure to warm up.

Now that you are familiar with what dynamic and static stretching are, let's take a look at why we warm up.

Chapter 4

Warming it Up: What's the Big Deal?

What's the difference between warming up and not warming up? Well, it's pretty much like the difference between cooked and uncooked spaghetti noodles. One is quite flexible and the other is not so much.

The bottom line is your body works better when it's warmed up. Like a spaghetti noodle, it bends better when it's warm. A car works best when it's warmed up, too. It operates best when you let the engine run a bit before driving it. Think about it. You never see a race car driver just hop in his car and take off. It's a given he will rev his engine up first.

Why? He wants to win.

WINNING REASONS TO WARM UP

- **Enhances Your Performance**

Just as a warmed up race car has a much better shot at winning, when your body is warmed up you will perform better, too. Not only will your body be more prepared, but your mindset will be, as well.

- ## Increases Blood Circulation

Did you know most of the capillaries (small blood vessels) within your muscles are closed until you begin to exercise? As you warm up, your blood circulation increases and they open up.

Since blood transports oxygen which fuels your muscles, it just makes sense you will do better all the way around when you warm up before a performance, workout, or competition.

- ## Heats Up Body Temperature

As your blood begins to flow, your muscles start to get warmer, literally. This causes the hemoglobin in your blood to put out more oxygen. Providing more oxygen to your muscles is like adding fuel to a fire which helps you blaze through your performance.

Not only does a warmer body temperature get your blood flowing and oxygen pumping, it also causes your muscles to contract and relax faster, increases nerve transmission, and optimizes muscle metabolism.

- ## Helps Prevent Injuries

You probably get tired of hearing it. No doubt, your dance instructor, gymnastics coach, or workout teacher has said it over and over. "Warming up helps prevent injuries."

It bears repeating though and has to be drilled into our heads because as artists and athletes, we want to get right down to business.

We run short on time or patience, and just want to jump into the action.

Why? Well, we're made that way.

For us, life isn't a spectator sport. No way. We want to be in the action. The truth of the matter is, warming up will help keep us in the action. It is a scientifically proven fact that warming up helps prevent injuries.

It takes more force to hurt a muscle once it has been warmed up. A warmed up muscle can withstand more stretching than a cold muscle can. A warm muscle is less likely to tear. It's worth the extra effort when you hate sitting on the sidelines.

- **Increases Flexibility**

Thinking back to the spaghetti noodle analogy, it's easy to see how warming up increases flexibility. When you do warm ups, your muscles literally heat up.

Just as hard noodles in a pot of boiling water do, your muscles begin to bend better as they get heated.

The more flexible your body becomes, the less likely you are to get injured and the better you are going to perform. Remember, the definition of flexibility is to bend, but not break which is certainly the object of the game.

- **Decreases Muscle Viscosity**

Muscle viscosity is a fancy term that simply means how effectively a muscle works. In between the layers of a muscle is a sac filled with fluid. The fluid lubricates the muscles and joints with a substance called synovial fluid. Synovial fluid keeps your muscles from reacting too quickly when they are being worked. It also slows the contraction of your muscle. Basically, it regulates how your muscles react and how quickly they do so. Your muscle viscosity is the measurement of how well the regulation is working.

If your muscle viscosity is too high, it is taking your body too long to lubricate the muscles, which can cause them to tear.

So, decreasing muscle viscosity is extremely important.

THE WINNING STRETCH

Stretching out *is* all it's cracked up to be.

So, the next time you are stretching, stretch to win.

Chapter 5
Cooling it Down: Stretching After Your Workout

After a strenuous workout, and especially after a performance, sometimes the last thing you want to do is to stretch out again.

You stretched before your workout. Isn't that good enough?

It's easy to skip the after stretches and get on home to your homework, your date, or whatever it is you have next on your busy list of things to do.

However, before you do, please remember, "It's not over until it's over." You won't regret taking some time to cool down. This is where you really increase your flexibility.

WHY STRETCH AFTER A WORKOUT?

There are a number of reasons to stretch after a workout and there is science behind it all. Here's what happens when you cool down:

- Your body recovers from the impact of major, quick movements.
- You allow your core body temperature to lower slowly.
- Your blood pressure is also allowed to decrease.
- Lactic acid is worked out of the muscles so they do not get as sore.
- Adrenaline begins to ebb from fight or flight mode.

FOCUS DURING YOUR COOL DOWN:

- **Slow Your Breathing and Lower Your Heart Rate**

When your body is in exercise mode, everything is working harder, especially your lungs and heart. They are desperately trying to deliver more blood and oxygen to your muscles and other parts of your body. This works out great while you are exerting energy and moving your arms, legs, and other parts of your body, but once the action slows, reduce your breathing.

- **Slowing Your Movement Down**

As you transition from your workout to your cool down, do it gradually. You don't want to shock your body by going from a full-throttle workout or performance to doing nothing at all.

Decrease your activity little by little and end up with cool down static stretches.

- **Hydration**

Dehydration can make you really sick and can actually be fatal. During a strenuous workout, your body requires more hydration than it does when you are not exercising, so be sure to drink plenty of water.

You will also find being hydrated gives you energy which you certainly need after a workout and it will also keep your muscles from cramping up and reduces soreness.

- **Increase Flexibility**

When your muscles are warm, they will stretch further. This is the perfect time to extend your muscles and increase your flexibility with static stretching.

KEY ELEMENTS OF A GREAT COOL DOWN

- Longer holds
- Gentle movements
- Refresh and refuel

USING STRETCH BANDS TO COOL DOWN

One of the best ways to cool down is to do static stretching. Ballet stretch bands are excellent to use for static cool down stretches.

Stretch bands help your muscles stretch. Since static stretches are passive or done without movement, the bands encourage your muscles to stretch through a process called resistance. Using a band adds a gentle tug to a normal stretch, which makes the exercise more effective.

Later in the book, you will find complete illustrated instructions on some great cool down static stretch exercises, so keep reading.

Chapter 6
How Muscles Work

If you are going to excel in ballet, it's important to get a basic understanding of how your muscles work. The more you know, the higher your chances of taking your skills to the next level. The same is true for any expression of the arts and in sports.

FIRST THINGS FIRST: WHAT IS A MUSCLE?

Muscles are soft tissues within the body that produce motion and force. Muscles are all made of a special type of elastic tissue similar to a rubber band. There are thousands of small fibers in every muscle.

There are three types of muscles: *smooth, skeletal, and cardiac.*

WHAT DO MUSCLES DO?

Muscles have a certain job to do or a specific role to play. Some have more than one purpose while others have many.

Cardiac muscles of the heart, pump blood in and out and also relax to let the chambers fill back up again.

Smooth muscles contract and make hollow organs work, like the gastrointestinal tract, blood vessels, bladder, and, in females, the uterus.

Skeletal muscles control movement of the body and can exert force. They are voluntary muscles, meaning you control them. They do things such as support your body posture, move your legs while dancing or other exercise, and curve your back when tumbling.

HOW MUSCLES WORK

Muscle cells have protein filaments containing actin and myosin that contract when they slide by each other. When this happens, the contraction changes the shape of the cell and the length, as well.

When the muscle is used in exercise it produces force and motion. When you rotate your legs in a dance, you are using the muscles in your external hip rotator and your gluteal muscles. Inside these two muscles, the filaments are contracting, enabling your muscles to contract which sets everything in motion and you are able to rotate your legs.

FASCINATING FACTS ABOUT MUSCLES

- There are about 650 skeletal muscles in your body.
- Your heart is made up of muscles.
- It takes only seventeen facial muscles to smile, but it requires the work of forty-three in order to frown.
- Muscles can only pull the end of muscles toward themselves (contracting), but cannot pull away from themselves.

HOW MUSCLES WORK WHEN IT COMES TO STRETCHING

Dynamic muscle contractions are used to do dynamic stretch exercises.

Remember, dynamic stretches are done with movement and control. When you do dynamic stretches, you are changing the length of your muscles and observable joint position (like your knee, for instance).

If you are squatting, your muscles must become shorter in order to lower you. If you are doing floor exercises and go to lift your foot up, your hamstring muscle must shorten so it can accomplish the task.

Static muscle contraction happens with the joints in place. Remember, static stretch exercises are done without motion. Your muscles are partially or fully contracting, but your joints are not moving. The torque (or measurement of force required to move your  muscles) is the same as the resistance. Meaning, you balance the amount of force with the amount of resistance so you are not moving your joints.

This is where resistance stretch bands come in to play. They apply more resistance so you can apply more force for an ultimate static stretch exercise.

TYPES OF MUSCLE CONTRACTIONS

Concentric: Concentric means to move toward the center. The movement of your muscle and the way you see your joint moving is toward the action.

When you leap, you are doing a concentric muscle contraction because your movement is in the direction of the action you are performing. The torque is the amount of force it takes to move these muscles.

Eccentric: Eccentric means to move away from the center. It is the lengthening of your muscles. If you are doing a leg lift, you use concentric muscle contraction to raise your leg up and you use eccentric muscle contraction to lower it back down.

23

Your muscles are lengthening in order to allow your leg to come back into place. This action can be done slowly or with holds in order to strengthen and challenge the muscle or muscles.

MORE ABOUT MUSCLES

- Agonists: These muscles make your joints move when they are contracted. They can be primary or secondary movers.

- Antagonists: These muscles have the opposite action of the muscle doing the major moving. They don't do any work unless they are needed to co-contract. If you are holding something up that needs to be stabilized, the antagonist muscles will kick into gear.

- Stabilizers: These muscles work to hold things in place when a force comes against them like gravity or a jolt. When a gymnast flips or tumbles, internal organs are held in place by these muscles.

- Synergists: These muscles cooperate and work alongside other muscles to achieve a goal.

Muscles are fascinating. The more you learn about them, the more you will become aware of them in your own personal workouts and performances.

As you direct your efforts and energies to the muscles you are using and understand how they work, you will no doubt find your use of them will improve.

Chapter 7
Myofascial Release

Myofascial release is a lot less complicated than it sounds. It is a therapy used in the medical field and in the sports and dance world that treats skeletal muscle immobility and pain. It reduces pain by relaxing the contracted muscles. It improves blood flow and can increase lymphatic circulation, by stimulating the stretch reflex.

Fascia is a soft tissue in the connective tissue which protects and gives support to our muscles. It can become tight or tense when overexerted, or when an injury occurs. The tightness causes stress and tension which prevents your blood from flowing freely to your muscle. Remember, your blood also carries oxygen to fuel your muscles.

Myofascial Release Can:

- Improve flexibility
- Alleviate or eliminate pain
- Restore motion
- Allow muscles to elongate
- Enhance strength
- Improve posture
- Promote movement awareness

- Protect muscles
- Release tension
- Break up scar tissue

HOW IS MYOFASCIAL RELEASE PERFORMED?

There are many ways myofascial release can be administered. Hospitals and doctors' offices are often set up with fancy equipment, as are sports therapy centers, that help stretch skeletal muscles and relax tight muscles. It can also be self-performed. Many dancers, gymnasts, and others who rely upon their muscles can benefit greatly from doing self-myofascial release techniques.

Dancing is one of the most strenuous performing arts there is. Gymnastics is said to be the most difficult sport in existence. Whether you are aspiring in one of those fields, are into another sport, or just want to work out to get in shape, you are probably going to run into sore muscles.

You may even overwork or injure yourself. Below are some things you can do in order to apply self-myofascial release:

Common Places You Can Apply Myofascial Release

- The back of your ankles and calves
- Your quads and back of your quads
- Your iliotibial band, the ligament that runs down the outside of the thigh from the hip to the shin
- Your back and shoulders
- The balls of your feet

Some Great Self-Myofascial Release Methods

- **Apply a Foam Roller**

  Foam rollers can be purchased or you can even make your own. There are many ways to make a foam roller and one of the simplest ways involves PVC pipe and a foam mat. You can find numerous ideas by Googling "how to make a foam roller."

  You can roll the roller over various muscles. The most common use is for tight legs and the calf muscle.

- **Tennis or Lacrosse Ball**

  You can simply roll a firm ball on the sore or injured area.

- **Theracane**

  The Theracane is an instrument which can be used in self-myofascial release to access hard to reach spots. It is shaped like a cane with curves so you can easily get to areas on your back and the back of your shoulders which often get stressed or injured.

- **Trigger Point Therapy Tools**

  These tools are designed to mimic the human hand and the healing touch can bring when applied in the right spot.

  When your muscles are tired or injured, they just don't work like they should. Plus, who wants to be uncomfortable or in pain?

  The next time you find your muscles could use some tender loving care, you might try self-myofascial release… your muscles will thank you for it.

Chapter 8
Check Yourself: Common Errors in Stretching

When it comes to stretching, it's best to check yourself before you wreck yourself. Stretching exercises are some of the most beneficial things you can do for your overall performance, but they can also be the most destructive.

Who wants to spend the time and effort doing something that causes more harm than good? No one does.

Please keep in mind, the purpose of this chapter is not to be critical. Performing artists and athletes are usually under a lot of pressure from instructors and coaches. They are also very critical about themselves.

If you are hard on yourself, give yourself a break. While the demands you put on your body can be the driving force to greatness, they can also hold you back. This chapter is designed to help you, not hurt you.

Remember, it's all about progress, not perfection. No dancer, gymnast, or athlete is perfect. We can strive for improvement, though. In doing so, here are some common mistakes you will want to avoid when stretching:

NOT PROPERLY WARMING UP

Cold muscles don't stretch well. Like that previously mentioned uncooked spaghetti noodle can easily break when bent, so can cold muscles.

Cold muscles that then get worked tend to be susceptible to injury. If you have thought stretching was the warm up, don't feel bad. It's a common misconception, but at least you know the truth now. Warming up *before* stretching is a must do.

NOT FOLLOWING A STRETCHING ROUTINE

Sometimes we run short on time or simply get so used to doing the same things over and over that we all get careless. It's a natural thing. However, at the same time, it can also be dangerous.

Have you ever gotten into your workout, kicked your leg up on the ballet barre only to realize, you didn't stretch your hamstrings?

Or, maybe you jumped down into the splits and remembered you hadn't done any middle split stretches. I don't have to tell you how that would work out.

The key is to follow a laid out plan each and every time you are going to put stress on your body. Your regime should include warming up and then stretching all of the muscles you will be using. If you do your routine often, you will avoid accidentally skipping a stretch.

NOT STRETCHING OFTEN ENOUGH

So, you warmed up, stretched, worked out, and then cooled down That is awesome and exactly what you should do.

However, as you know, many in the performing arts and sports world tend to take training to the limit. You are back for yet another workout or maybe even a performance. Surely, you don't have to take the time to do the routine all over again. Or do you?

The bad news is yes, you do. But, the bad news is also the good news. By warming up and doing your stretching exercises again, you are double ready. You can go into your performance, workout, or competition knowing you are fully prepared to do your ultimate best.

Then, don't forget to cool down again when you finish. Hey, if doing what you do was easy, everyone would do it. They don't, but you do.

PUTTING TOO MUCH WEIGHT ON YOUR JOINTS AND JOINT CAPSULES

Your joints are amazing things. They have joint capsules which surround them much like an envelope. The joint capsules have two layers. One is the outer fibrous layer, which is a fibrous membrane that forms the joint capsule and houses the synovial layer. The synovial layer is the inner membrane. The synovial membranes hold and secrete synovial fluid to protect the joint.

The joint capsules provide both active and passive stability. They help your body to balance and not cave in when doing something like standing, jumping, and lifting.

It is important not to put too much weight on your joints and joint capsules or you will damage them. Then, you are in real trouble. Some dance routines, especially ice-dancing routines, require one dancer to lift another. This movement could put too much weight on the joints. It also requires a lot of preparation and consideration before attempting. You can also put too much resistance on your joints when stretching.

PUTTING TOO MUCH PRESSURE ON YOUR LIGAMENTS

When you stretch, the idea is to elongate your muscles. However, in doing so, your ligaments can become stretched out, which is known as excessive ligament looseness or ligamentous laxity.

As you may have guessed, this is not a good thing. The condition can compress your nerves which causes discomfort and pain and can also result in walking, standing, or moving abnormally.

To avoid this, be sure not to hold your joints in any position that puts too much pressure or weight on them when you are stretching.

NOT STRETCHING WITH SLOW, SMOOTH MOVEMENTS

Stretching is to be done with no movement (static) or with slow, smooth, controlled movements (dynamic). If you are being too rough in your stretching, such as moving too haphazardly or too fast, you risk hurting yourself to the point where you are sidelined.

Never force a stretch. Never do it to the point of pain. Pay close attention to your range of motion to make sure it's within your body's comfort zone. Do these things and you will be fine.

NOT STRETCHING TO FULL EXTENSION

It's important to stretch to your full extension. It's understandable to be cautious after reading how overstretching can be dangerous, but getting into a complete stretch is equally as important.

An incorrect, partial stretch can be damaging, too. In order to avoid this, simply control your speed through your entire range of motion so you feel the stretching, but it is not painful.

Go a bit further each time being sure to complete the stretch, but never pushing it to the point of pain or discomfort.

FLEXIBILITY IS NOT WHAT YOU MIGHT THINK... THAT MISCONCEPTION IS A MISTAKE

A lot of people who get into ballet, dance, gymnastics, or cheerleading do so because they are flexible. Their bodies simply bend easily. You may be one of those types. If so, fantastic. It gives you an upper edge when doing such activities as the splits, tumbling, and balance beam. Beware, though. Being flexible does not mean you don't need to stretch. Nor does it mean you need to stretch less.

Remember, it's a long stretch to the top... we'll help you get there. Inch by inch, precept by precept. Everything you are doing is taking you forward. Even making mistakes. After all, if you're not making a few mistakes along the way, chances are you're still in your comfort zone.

Chapter 9
Looping It All Together: The Big Picture

We've covered a lot of information. Congratulations for sticking with it this far. Your stick-to-itiveness (yes, it's a real word in the dictionary) will get you far.

Now, it's time to get all the pieces of the puzzle into place so you can put what you have learned into action. As cheerleaders say, "Ready? Okay!"

PRELIMINARIES

There are a few things to remember. You probably know them already, but they are super important, so here's a quick summary:

- If you are sick or injured, take a breather from your activities and when you feel better, start up again gradually.
- Focus on progress, not perfection. Stretch wisely.
- Be sure to wear appropriate clothing that stretches and moves *with* you.
- If you are stretching with resistance equipment, like a ballet stretch band, be sure you use a high-quality one so it doesn't snap.
- Don't forget to reward yourself for a job well done.

WARMING UP

Remember the spaghetti noodle? Warming up before you stretch makes great sense when you think about a noodle and how brittle it is before it's heated and how flexible it is afterward. The same is true with your muscles and your whole body for that matter.

Warm ups really do *warm* your body up. It's not just a cute term to use for the exercises done before stretching. Warm ups not only get your body temperature to rise, they also:

- Increase your heart and respiratory rates.
- Boost the amount of oxygen and nutrients to your muscles.
- Prepare you mentally for your workout or performance.
- Help prevent injuries.
- Elevate your capabilities.
- Get you physically prepared for strenuous, demanding activity.

Some important things to keep in mind are:

- Practice good posture while you are warming up.
- Focus on your abdominal control to help keep your spine aligned.
- Breathe regularly to get oxygen flowing to your muscles. Never hold your breath.

Types of Warm Ups

There are a number of warm ups you can do to serve the purpose of preparing your body for stretching and then for your workout. The type of warm ups you will do and what muscles you want to focus on depends on the kind of workout you will be doing.

Ballet dancers often use different muscles than those folks who are warming up to run a marathon. With your workout goal in mind, think of the muscles you will be using and chose accordingly.

You can jog in place, do arm circles, leg circles, and so on. A swimmer might want to take a few light laps around the pool. Taking the muscles you are going to use into a full range of motion is a must.

Don't be afraid to warm up muscles you don't plan to be using. You can never warm up too much.

Now that you are good and warm, here is a review of stretching and some new information.

STRETCH EXERCISES

Stretching is done to limber you up and get your muscles ready so they can do more, be stronger, faster, and go through all you put them through in your intense workout performance.

It is during stretching that you get your blood circulating, which in turn gets oxygen to your muscles, fueling them to do their thing.

When it comes to stretching, remember there are two basic kinds: static, which is done without moving your joints, and dynamic, which is done with movement.

Stretching can be done by simply stretching the areas you want to limber up, like spreading your legs toward the middle splits and holding it. The middle splits are the ultimate stretch and are accomplished by spreading the legs while sitting on the ground into a 180-degree angle. These mean spreading the legs until they are in line with each other and extended in opposite directions. It can also be accomplished by adding resistance. Resistance is something that pulls or gives tension in the opposite direction.

There are different methods of resistance stretching and different equipment to help you as well. One of the best ways to do get resistance is by using a stretch band, also called a ballet stretch band or resistance band. They are similar to a giant rubber band and are stretchy. They come in different sizes, colors, strengths, and above all, different qualities.

A Few Things Stretching With a Stretch Band Does:

- De-sensitizes the protective mechanism that keeps your muscles from fully extending.
- Increases flexibility in your muscles and joints.
- Maximizes muscle strength.
- Optimizes muscle function.
- Provides rapid gains in your stretching ability.

With that in mind, here are some points to when using a resistance stretch band.

- Even when using a stretch band, static stretch exercises are still done without moving your joints. To do otherwise can really hurt you.
- The stretch bands are designed to help your muscles stretch further and to work harder, so keep in mind, when using one, you are pushing your muscles further than you do when in the same position without the bands.

- Easy does it. You can build up to stretching further and longer, but don't overdo it or you will be going backward.

STRETCHING YOUR LIMITS

While regular stretch exercises make you more flexible because they reduce tension in your muscles, stretch bands and other resistance equipment methods do more than simply relax and lengthen the muscles and connective tissues.

They actually break down things that can greatly inhibit stretching like scar tissue, muscle fiber build-up (fascia), and built up adhesions.

COOLING IT DOWN

Ahhhh… the cool down. You're in the home stretch, so don't give up now. I know, it's tempting to drop from exhaustion or rush on home or wherever your next stop is, but it's like a baseball player not touching home plate, you won't win the game without completing it.

Here's What a Cool Down Does:

- Decreases your heart rate
- Normalizes your breathing
- Decreases your adrenaline
- Brings your body temperature back to normal

MEDICAL FACTS TO BACK IT UP

Seriously, it's a big deal to cool down. When you put your body through a strenuous workout, competition, or performance, it is locked into fight or flight mode. That is something instilled in all of us.

It's designed to help us in times of danger. You have heard of the stories, such as a man who lifted a car off a person it had fallen onto or the elderly woman who drove away a would-be burglar.

How could they do such heroic feats?

Adrenaline. It pumps through our body to give us the extra measure needed to get out of danger, Adrenaline also gives us an extra push to make it through a good workout, performance, race, or sports event. It's a good thing, but too much of a good thing is not good at all.

When you are working your body to its limit, you increase the blood flow so more can circulate to your legs, feet, arms, hands, and the muscles associated with them. The blood vessels expand to let this blood through.

When you suddenly stop exercising and don't let them gradually get back to normal, the blood can get pooled in your lower body, thus cutting it off from properly flowing to your upper body, like your head.

WAYS TO COOL DOWN

Cooling down the muscles you worked is best because those are the ones that are elongated and need to go back into position. Of course, just like in your warm up, it never hurts to cool your whole body down, but if you are selecting a muscle group, don't leave out those you just worked.

Runners like to cool down by jogging and gradually decreasing to a fast walk, then a slower walking pace. Swimmers may do the same with swimming movements. Ballet dancers can gradually work the muscles they worked during their performance or workout.

In addition to cooling off by repeating the movement you were doing during your workout just doing it slower and with less force, you can also do cool down stretches. These can be done with or without the use of a stretch band. Keep reading for some excellent instructions on specific warm up and cool down stretches.

Chapter 10
Cool Tips and Hot Warm-Ups

By now, you understand that a couple of quick stretches on the barre is not enough to constitute a warm up. Neither is a few tumbles down the gym mat or a herkie before you run out onto the football field.

Warming up is serious business. It can keep you from getting hurt and can also help you perform at your best. In other words, warm ups are cool when you get right down to it.

Arm Roll Outs

Rolling out your arms does a number of beneficial things to warm your body up. It gets your blood circulating, which means more fuel is going to your muscles.

It causes your arm muscles to begin to actually heat up a bit, so they are more flexible and it will also warm up your shoulders, increasing the range of motion in the joints.

1. Stand straight and tall with your arms to your side.
2. Bring your arms out to your side, up even with your shoulders.
3. Roll them forward ten times and then backward ten times.
4. Repeat ten times.

Jumping Jacks

Let's get that blood pumping! Jumping jacks are a fantastic way to raise your core temperature, which gets everything moving and warmed up.

1. Stand with your feet close together, arms to your sides.
2. Tighten your abdominal muscles so your pelvis is forward and your lower back is straight.
3. Slightly bend your knees.
4. Now, jump so you land with your feet a bit over a shoulder's width apart.
5. At the same time, raise your arms above your head. (You should be on the balls of your feet.)
6. With your knees slightly bent, jump again, as you bring your feet together and your arms back to your sides.
7. Repeat fifteen times.

Rolling It Back and Rolling It Up

This exercise will help your body establish balance and mobility in the neck, back, spine, and hamstrings. It will warm up your abdominal muscles, get your blood circulating, relieve tension, create space between the vertebrae, and promote proper posture as well.

1. Drop your chin to your chest.
2. Roll through your back reaching your hands to the floor.
3. When you feel the need, bend your knees.
4. Stretch and hold.
5. Slowly, go all the way back up to a standing position.
6. Repeat five to ten times.

Neck and Shoulder Roll

In one way or another, any workout or performance you do will use your neck and/or your shoulders.

In ballet, even your arm positions will use these muscles. In cheerleading, your arm movements rely heavily upon your neck and shoulders. The strain often placed on the neck and shoulders when doing gymnastics is immense.

Not warming up your neck and shoulders properly can lead to serious injury, so be sure to take the time to do these warm ups, no matter what sport or performing art you are doing.

1. Stand with your feet shoulder-width apart.
2. Slowly tilt your head to the side. Gently pull.
3. Repeat on the other side.

Take Time for the Spine

The health of your spine is crucial, not just in the performing arts and in sports, but for your life in general. The spine is the second most injured body part in dancers, preceded only by leg injuries. It is a leading injury in gymnasts.

Spinal injuries can lead to chronic pain. Here's a warm up to help make sure your spine is prepared.

1. Kneel on the floor on your hands and knees with your palms directly under your shoulders and your knees under your hip bones. Your fingers will be pointed away from you.
2. Tuck in your chin, and then curve your back upward toward the ceiling. Gently pull.
3. Arch your back, pulling your head up toward the ceiling.
4. Tilt your tailbone up.
5. Return to your original position and repeat five times.

Hip Warm Ups

Warm ups are hip, literally. The hip is another part of the body widely used in ballet, dance, gymnastics, and most any other performing art or sport. You will need a lot of hips flexibility.

Did you know a turnout, the classic ballet starting position with toes  and knees turned out and heels together, requires the work of six muscles located deep within your pelvic and hip area?

The hips are often overworked in many of the performing arts and in sports, as well. Make sure to warm them up each and every time.

1. Lay down on your back.
2. Pull your right knee to your chest.
3. Circle your bent leg out to the side.
4. Return your leg next to your other leg, lengthwise.
5. Repeat ten times.
6. Switch and do the same using your left leg.

Ankle Rotation Sensation

It goes without saying that your ankles need to be warmed up. Just think of how much weight is put on them just by walking. It is very important to get them ready to roll or not to roll.

1. Lay on the floor.
2. Gently point the toe of your right foot.
3. Lift your right leg slightly off the floor.

4. Rotate your ankle in a circle.
5. Repeat ten times to the right and ten times to the left.
6. Now, do the same on your left side.

Back Legs and Hips Dip

We've talked about how important it is to warm up the hips, but the hamstrings (back of the legs) are super significant too.

1. With your legs wide apart and your feet pointed out, bend your knees.
2. Drop your hips down to the floor to a deep, wide squat.
3. From there, bring one leg out straight to the side as you stretch.

4. Hold for twenty seconds.
5. With your hands, walk yourself to the other side and repeat.
6. Do both sides ten times.

Jogging in Place

This is a very simple warm up, but one that does so much. This will actually begin to set your body temperature even higher, so it will be ready for the activity which lies ahead.

You will also begin to increase your heart rate. Although it's super easy, it's important to do it correctly, practicing good posture, and breathing regularly.

1. With your arms to your side, take a deep, slow breath.
2. Gently begin to jog in place for ten steps on each foot.
3. Gradually pump up the pace ten more steps.
4. Go one more round, even faster.
5. Gradually cool down your pace.
6. End with your arms beside you in a standing position.

THE SCIENCE: What Warming Up Really Does

- Heats your body to a warmer temperature preparing the muscles for stretching.
- Increases the range of movement of your joints.
- Increases the extensibility of your muscles, ligaments connective tissues, and tendons.
- Releases stored fuel for energy.

- Moves your body from a relative rest state to an active state.
- Changes your nervous system from parasympathetic to sympathetic control (basically the fight or flight that pumps adrenaline and strength, great for competitions and peak performances).
- Circulates and redistributes blood.

HOT WARM UP TIPS

- Remember, warm ups are literally for warming your body up. Especially if you're warming up where it's cold, add extra layers of clothing to get a jump start on the process.
- Warming up is not only for your body, but for your mind, as well. Surround yourself with positive things like motivational posters, inspiring music, and anything else that pumps you up.
- Focus on the muscles you will be using because those are the ones you want to be sure get warmed up. Warming up muscles you won't use is sweet, too, like icing on the cake.
- Did you know during a warm up, your body's digestive system shuts down to supply your muscles with more blood? Eating during a warm up is definitely not a good idea.
- The object of warming up is to get your body gradually used to the strenuous workout or performance ahead, so easy does it.

Chapter 11
Chill Out With These Cool Downs

You've completed your workout or your award-winning performance. Now, it's time to reward your body for a job well done.

Not cooling down is like denying a kid a lollipop after getting a shot at the doctor's office with no tears shed. Or like getting a great report card, but nobody recognizes it.

Your body deserves to get what it craves which is to recover by way of a great cool down.

A GOOD COOL DOWN:

- Gradually decreases your heart rate.
- Gradually decreases your body temperature.
- Allows blood circulation to return to the places it decreases in when strenuously exercising, like the digestive organs.
- Gives your mind a chance to refocus.
- Prevents your blood from pooling in your feet and legs which can lead to fainting.

COOL DOWN EXERCISES

Roll It Up

It's time to roll it up, literally. As you begin to calm your body from its hard work back to a normally functioning zone, the same rolling exercises you used to get warmed up are perfect for cooling down, as well.

1. Stand with your arms beside your body.
2. Roll your neck with your chin to your chest.
3. Roll your back all the way down, touching your hands to the floor.
4. Now, roll your back all the way back up.
5. Repeat ten times.

Side Swipe

If you've ever gotten a cramp in your side, you will appreciate the importance of this cool down exercise.

Remember, your circulation is greatly slowed to your digestive area during your workout, and afterward, the blood attempts to flow there again, so help it along its way with this must do exercise.

1. Stand with your feet about a shoulder's width apart.
2. Raise your right hand above your head and reach to the side as you stretch to the left.

3. Slightly roll your back around and come back to the above stance.
4. Press down to the left to increase your side stretch.
5. Hold for ten seconds and come up to your original position.
6. Repeat ten times on the other side.

Back Thigh Stretch

Chances are, the workout or routine has placed a pretty good strain on your thighs. You have elongated them, so now it's time to get them back to their comfort zone.

1. With your feet in a wide stance, turned to the side with toe to heel, turn your body to face the side, toes pointing forward.
2. Roll forward with your back, touching your hands to the ground or if that is too intense, touch your shin instead.
3. Stretch your back and the back of your legs.
4. Hold for twenty to thirty seconds while you breathe deeply and relax the back of your thighs.
5. Return to side stance position.
6. Repeat five to ten times.
7. Repeat on the other side.

Runner's Lunge

This exercise will stretch the front of your hips.

1. Stand with your legs a shoulder's width apart, with the toes of your right foot pointing toward the heel of your left foot, like you are gearing up for a race.

2. Lunge downward with your left knee bent, allowing your right leg to stretch out behind you.
3. Keep your left foot flat on the floor and your left knee bent and positioned directly above your left foot.
4. Keep your back and your right outstretched leg as straight as possible, so the muscles stretch into a relaxed state.
5. Hold for twenty to thirty seconds.

Getting a Toe Hold on Cooling Down

Did you know each of your feet contains twenty-six bones, over a hundred tendons, and thirty-three joints?

Cracks, breaks, and Achilles tendonitis are all complications of the feet resulting from the strain put on them, especially during ballet performances and gymnastic meets. Take care of your feet and they will take care of you.

1. Sit on the floor with your legs extended straight out in front of you, taking care to keep your posture good.
2. Gently flex your feet up toward you.

3. Reach forward to touch your toes.
4. Clasp your hands and place them behind your feet.
5. Stretch and hold for ten to twenty seconds, breathing deeply and feeling the stretch.
6. Repeat ten times.

Modified Pigeon Stretch

This is a fantastic cool down for your upper inner thighs. Don't skip this one, as it helps align the muscles you have stretched.

1. Sit with your back straight and shoulders aligned.
2. Extend your left leg in front of you with your leg bent.
3. Extend your right leg behind you with knee bent.
4. With your spine straight, slowly walk yourself over your left leg until you are leaning on your elbows.
5. Hold for twenty to thirty seconds.
6. Come back up into your original sitting position.
7. Change sides and repeat.

HOT TIPS FOR YOUR COOL DOWN

- Do cool down your entire body after focusing on specific muscles.
- Be sure to cool down enough. Don't rush a good thing.
- You should feel your heart rate slowing down gradually.
- You should also feel your breathing come back to normal.

Remember... A Proper Cool Down Prevents a Meltdown.

Chapter 12
Step-by-Step Stretch Band Instructions

STRETCHES FROM THE BUTTERFLY POSITION

Butterfly Stretch

1. Sit on the floor in the butterfly position with your back straight and shoulders down

2. Loop one end of the stretch band around the center of your right foot. Bring the band behind your back where it falls above your hips.

3. Loop the left end of the band around the center of your left foot. Gently pull your heels toward you.

4. Use your elbows to push your legs toward the floor.

5. Breathe deep and hold the pose for twenty to thirty seconds while concentrating on your breathing and the muscles you are stretching.

6. Relax for ten to twenty seconds. Repeat two times.

Side Stretch

1. Sit on the floor in the butterfly position with your back straight.

2. Place the band around your waist and loop it around each foot.

3. Bend your knees and let them fall to the ground. Hold your left arm above your head and stretch your side with your right palm placed on the floor behind your right knee.

4. Hold the pose for twenty to thirty seconds while concentrating on your breathing and the muscles you are stretching.

5. Relax for twenty seconds. Repeat two times.

Side Hamstring Stretch

1. From the butterfly position, slowly stretch your left leg out to the side, where it is even with your left hip. Keep your knee straight and your toes pointed up. Your right knee will be bent into your body.

2. With your back straight and your shoulders aligned forward, allow the band to pull your leg gently off the floor and hold.

3. Breathe deep. Hold the pose for twenty to thirty seconds while concentrating on your breathing and the muscles you are stretching.

4. Relax for ten to twenty seconds. Repeat two times.

Side Hamstring Stretch with Bend

1. From the side hamstring stretch position, place the palms of your hands on the floor on either side of your left leg, just below your knee.

2. Slowly allow your foot to be pulled up by the band.

3. Hold the pose for twenty to thirty seconds while concentrating on your breathing and the muscles you are stretching.

4. Relax for twenty seconds. Repeat two times.

Hamstring and Side Stretch

1. From the side hamstring stretch position, stretch your right side by stretching your right arm and hand up and over toward your left leg.

2. Hold the pose for twenty to thirty seconds while concentrating on your breathing and the muscles you are stretching.

3. Relax for twenty seconds. Repeat two times.

Hamstring and Back Stretch

1. From the side hamstring stretch position, slightly turn and look to your right side with your head turned to the right and the back side of your right hand touching your lower back.

2. Gently lift your left foot up while holding the top of your foot with your left hand.

3. Hold the pose for twenty to thirty seconds while concentrating on your breathing and the muscles you are stretching.

4. Relax for twenty seconds. Repeat two times.

Calf Stretch with Foot Hold

1. From the side hamstring stretch position, rest your right hand on your right knee while facing your left leg. Bend your right leg as far as possible, bracing it against the straight left leg.

2. Gently lift your foot up, holding the top of it with your left hand.

3. Hold for twenty to thirty seconds while concentrating on the muscles your stretching

4. Relax for twenty seconds. Repeat two times.

5. Repeat on the opposite side.

Calf Stretch Sitting Tall With a Band

1. Sit on the floor.

2. Loop one end of the band around your right foot.

3. Bend your right knee and place the sole of your right foot on your inner thigh.

4. Wrap the band around your waist in the back and extend it to where it is looped around your left foot.

5. Flex your left foot toward you while holding the band with your right hand above your left knee.

6. Place your left hand on your lower hip.

7. Slightly lift the band up so your lower calf and foot are off the ground. You should feel a slight stretch.

8. Hold for ten seconds.

9. Repeat two times.

10. Switch sides and repeat.

Calf Stretch Using Band

1. From the side hamstring stretch position take hold of the loop on your left foot and gently pull your body toward your knee.

2. Hold the pose for twenty to thirty seconds while concentrating on your breathing and the muscles you are stretching.

3. Relax for seconds. Repeat two times.

4. Switch and repeat on the opposite side.

Middle Splits

1. The middle split is the ultimate in stretching. Sit on the floor with your back straight and your shoulders aligned.

2. Attach the band to your right foot and get in the side hamstring stretch position.

3. Gently stretch your left legs into the middle split position, as pictured, and place your palms on the floor directly in front of you. Hold the pose for twenty to thirty seconds while concentrating on your breathing and the muscles you are stretching.

4. Relax for twenty seconds. Repeat two times.

Lying Forward in Middle Splits

1. This stretch takes the middle splits to the limit. After you have completed the middle split exercise above, lean forward with your chest touching the floor in front of you.

2. Bend your elbows and place your hands under your chin. Hold for twenty to thirty seconds while someone snaps your picture!

3. Relax for twenty seconds. Repeat two times.

FRONT SPLIT STRETCHES

Half Front Split

1. Start in the butterfly position, but put the strap on your right shoulder instead of your right foot. Place the other end on the left foot.

2. Slowly extend your left leg backward into a half split.

3. Stretch your left leg out behind you with a slight bend of your knee. Hold your left arm up above your head.

4. Hold the pose for twenty to thirty seconds while concentrating on your breathing and the muscles you are stretching.

5. Relax for twenty seconds. Repeat two times.

6. Switch and repeat on the opposite side.

Half Splits with Quadriceps Stretch

1. Sit on the floor and double loop the band around your left foot, then loop it once around your right upper foot and position it so it goes over your shoulder from one foot to the other.

2. As you assume the front split position, bend your left leg and raise your foot up and slightly to the right.

3. Stretch your right leg up slightly off the floor. Place your palms on the floor on either side of your upper left leg.

4. Hold the pose for twenty to thirty seconds while concentrating on your breathing and the muscles you are stretching.

5. Relax for twenty seconds. Repeat two times.

6. Switch and repeat on the opposite side.

Half Splits Strength Work

1. Sit on the floor and loop the band around your left foot once. Slowly bring it over your shoulder and loop around your right upper foot. Position it so it goes over your shoulder from one foot to the other.

2. As you assume the front split position, bend your left leg. It will raise slightly. You can work on strength by trying to push it down into a full front split or hold it for flexibility in the front split position.

3. Place your palms on the floor on either side of your upper left leg.

4. Hold the pose for twenty to thirty seconds while concentrating on your breathing and the muscles you are stretching.

5. Relax for twenty seconds. Repeat two times.

6. Switch and repeat on the opposite side.

Front Splits

1. Start in the butterfly position, but put the strap on your right shoulder and on your left foot.

2. Slowly, extend your left leg backward into a half split.

3. Slowly, extend your front leg into the full front splits.

4. Place your palms on the floor on either side of your right outstretched leg.

5. Point your toes and hold for twenty to thirty seconds while concentrating on your breathing and the muscles you are stretching.

6. Relax for twenty seconds. Repeat two times.

7. Switch and repeat on the opposite side.

LUNGE EXERCISES

Kneeling Quadriceps Stretch

1. Stand with your legs a hip-width apart.

2. Loop the band around the middle of your left foot, and then bring it over your right shoulder.

3. Step forward with your right leg and plant your left knee on the floor so it is bent and your right foot is on the ground.

4. With your left hand on the floor, lower your body to where your front left thigh is parallel to the floor. At this point, the stretch band should be snug.

5. Hold for twenty to thirty seconds while concentrating on your breathing and the muscles you are stretching.

6. Relax twenty seconds. Repeat two times.

7. Switch and repeat on the opposite side.

Arms Overhead Quadriceps Stretch

1. This is another lunge that will stretch your hamstrings as well as your back, shoulders, and arms. Perform the kneeling quadriceps stretch then step forward with your left leg.

2. Hold the band with both hands and stretch with arms extended above your head with your back straight, stretching upward.

3. Hold the pose for twenty to thirty seconds while concentrating on your breathing and the muscles you are stretching.

4. Relax for twenty seconds. Repeat two times.

5. Switch and repeat on the opposite side.

STANDS WITH THE BAND

Holding Leg Lift

1. Stand facing the back of a chair and place your right hand on it. Loop the middle of the stretch band around your left leg. It should twist around your left knee and attach to your left foot. The other end will loop around your right shoulder.

2. Extend your left leg out to a ninety-degree angle while keeping your right hand on the chair and your left arm out in front of you.

3. Hold for twenty to thirty seconds while concentrating on your breathing and the muscles you are stretching.

4. Relax for twenty seconds. Repeat two times.

5. Switch and repeat on the opposite side.

Standing Front Split

This stretch is great to flex out your inner and outer thighs. It's also fantastic for your shoulders, arms, and back and helps your balance, as well.

1. Stand straight facing a chair.

2. Hold the band with your right hand, wrapping it around your wrist once.

3. Take the other end of the band over your right shoulder and loop it around your left foot.

4. Hold onto the chair with your left hand.

5. Lean forward toward the chair, slightly arching your back.

6. As you are leaning in, bring your left foot up over your head so you are basically doing the split in the air.

7. Slowly lower your left foot back to the ground while bringing your torso back to a standing position.

8. Hold for twenty to thirty seconds while concentrating on your breathing and the muscles you are stretching.

9. Repeat two times.

10. Switch sides and repeat.

Lord of the Dance Stretch

1. Wrap the band around your left foot. Stand on your right leg.

2. Hold the ends of the band with your hands held above your head and back a bit with your back arched slightly.

3. Lift your right leg up, and apply tension to the band. Your knee will be slightly bent and your foot will point toward the ceiling.

4. Hold for twenty to thirty seconds while concentrating on your breathing and the muscles you are stretching.

5. Return your left foot to the ground.

6. Repeat two times.

7. Work the other side.

Forward Facing Front Split

1. Stand with your right side facing a chair.

2. Hold on to the chair with your left hand with your elbow bent, arm crossing your upper abdomen.

3. Double loop your band around your right hand and your left foot.

4. Bring your right hand to the top of your head so your left foot is even with your head and the tension can be felt from the band.

5. Your right foot should remain on the ground.

6. Hold for ten seconds, while relaxing and concentrating on the muscles you are stretching.

7. Release and repeat two times.

8. Repeat on the opposite side.

Holding Leg Lift Floor Touch

1. Stand facing the back of the chair. Double the band over your left foot and hold it with your right fist.

2. Keep your right foot on the floor and your right leg straight while lifting your left leg up, bending it at the knee.

3. Hold the chair with your left hand while pressing your right hand with the band downward.

4. Hold the pose for twenty to thirty seconds while concentrating on your breathing and the muscles you are stretching.

5. Relax for twenty seconds. Repeat two times.

6. Repeat on the opposite side.

Standing Front Split

1. Stand with your left side facing a chair.

2. Hold on to the chair with your left arm. Slightly bend you arm at the elbow and hold the chair with your left hand.

3. Loop the band around your right hand and around your lef foot.

4. Raise your right hand up beside your head with your elbow bent.

5. Pull your leg up over your head with your feet pointed.

6. Hold for thirty seconds, while relaxing and concentrating on the muscles being stretched.

7. Repeat two times.

8. Repeat on the opposite side.

Ballerina Pose

1. Loop the band around your right shoulder.

2. Bring the band across your shoulder, down your back and loop it around your left foot.

3. Hold your right arm out and your left arm forward and up as you bring your left foot back with a steady, slow motion.
4. Hold for ten seconds. Relax and concentrate on the muscles you are stretching.

5. Repeat two times.

6. Work on the opposite side.

En Pointe with Stretch Bands

1. Stand facing the back of a chair.

2. Loop the band across your right shoulder, bring it across your back, and loop it around your left foot.

3. Stand en pointe on your right foot. This is where you stand on the tip of your toes.

4. Reach to touch the floor with your right hand with the band is still around your right shoulder.

5. Hold for ten seconds. Relax on concentrate on the muscles you are stretching.

6. Resume a standing position.

7. Repeat two times.

8. Repeat on the opposite side.

Back Leg Lift

1. Place the band around your right shoulder and left foot.

2. Stand on your right foot.

3. Bring your left leg out to the side and back.

4. Keep your arms in the fifth arm position. Raise both arms over your head forming an oval, with your hands almost touching.

5. Hold for ten seconds while concentrating on your breathing and the muscles you are stretching.

6. Return to standing position.

7. Repeat two times.

8. Repeat on the opposite side.

Standing Quadriceps Stretch

1. The next stretch can be done using a wall, a chair, or anything stable. Loop the band around the top of your right foot then over your right shoulder and hold it in your left hand.

2. Bend your right leg up at the knee and slightly apply tension to the strap. With your left leg straight and planted on the ground, rest your right hand on the wall.

3. Turn your neck to the left so it stretches slightly.

4. Hold the pose for twenty to thirty seconds while concentrating on your breathing and the muscles you are stretching.

5. Relax for twenty seconds. Repeat two times.

Balancing Standing Quadriceps Stretch

1. Get into the s quadriceps stretch.

2. Push off the wall.

3. Hold for twenty-second. Relax and concentrate on the muscles you are stretching.

4. Repeat two times.

5. Repeat for the opposite side.

LOWER BACK STRETCHES

Stretch Band Leg Press from Ground

1. Lie flat on the floor with the middle of the band behind your back at the arch and the ends looped twice around your left foot. Your right leg should be straight.

2. Push your left leg up and hold on to the band with one hand on each side.

3. Hold the pose for twenty to thirty seconds while concentrating on your breathing and the muscles you are stretching.

4. Relax for twenty seconds. Repeat two times.

5. Repeat for the opposite leg.

Lower Back Stretch Toes Pointed

1. Lay on the floor with your legs straight down. Wrap the band around your right foot.

2. Extend your right leg up in the air. Slowly, straighten your right leg.

3. Point your toe once you reach your ultimate stretch. You can also pull toward your chest for an added stretch.

4. Hold the pose for twenty to thirty seconds while concentrating on your breathing and the muscles you are stretching.

5. Relax for twenty-seconds. Repeat two times.

6. Repeat on the opposite side.

Stretch Band Leg Press for Strength

1. Sit on the floor with your back straight and shoulders aligned.

2. Wrap the band around your back about mid-back

3. Loop both ends around the middle of your left foot. Place your right leg on the floor with your knee bent. Your right foot should be under your left thigh.

4. Slowly extend your left leg. Your palms should be on the floor behind your buttocks with your fingers pointing toward your body.

5. Hold the pose for twenty to thirty seconds. Relax and concentrate on the muscles you are stretching.

6. Relax for twenty seconds. Repeat two times.

7. Repeat on the opposite side.

Stretching the Core

Flex your arch.

It's important for the arch of your back to undergo some serious stretching because of all things, you don't want your back to be whacked out of alignment.

1. Lay on the floor on your stomach.

2. Wrap one end of the stretch band around both feet so it comes up between your feet.

3. Grab the other end with your hands.

4. Stretch your upper body upward and back as you lift your feet and lower legs upward.

5. Hold the band with enough tension to give a nice stretch.

6. Hold ten seconds. Relax and concentrate on the muscles you are stretching.

7. Go back to your original position, lying flat on the floor on your stomach.

8. Repeat two times.

CHEERLEADING BONUS STRETCHES

This exercise requires stretching and some balance, perfect for ballet and gymnastics, too.

1. Place both band loops on your left foot and hold the middle with your right hand.

2. Stand with your right leg planted firmly on the ground. Lift your left leg into the air while holding the band with your right hand

3. For a cool pose, put the left arm out straight.

4. Work up to holding the pose for twenty to thirty seconds while concentrating on your breathing and the muscles you are stretching.

5. Relax for twenty-seconds. Repeat two times.

6. Repeat for the opposite side.

This stretch is great for your back as well as strengthening your legs and stomach.

1. Loop the middle of the band around the outer part of your left ankle and hold the ends with your hands, one end in each hand.

2. Slowly, pull your left leg behind you. Your body should be leaning forward and your arms over your head with your hands slightly back as they hold the band.

3. Hold the pose for twenty to thirty seconds. Relax and concentrate on the muscles you are stretching.

4. Relax for twenty seconds. Repeat two times.

Chapter 13
Here's To Your Success!

Congratulations! I knew you could do it. Even if you haven't *done* all the things in the book yet, you've at least read through it and you know more about stretching than you did before.

That's a start and you know what they say, "In order to get anywhere, you must first get started." And… you are getting somewhere. You are getting to the top. Remember, we're going to help you get there.

Bumps Along the Way

If you are going to stretch yourself to the top, there are bound to be bumps along the way. If you are one who is determined to excel, chances are you are pretty hard on yourself at times, maybe all the time.

You probably set high demands and get mad at yourself when you don't achieve them. Please keep in mind it's not how many times you fall; it's how many times you get back up.

Failure is never final. Keep your chin up and give yourself a break.

Commitment Makes Your Dream a Reality

When you are doing what you love, it should be a joy, not a pain. If you are serious about dancing, ballet, or whatever moves you, be sure you have a passion for it or it will be hard to give all it takes to be successful. If you do love it that much, it will require commitment.

It's like the story about Farmer Jones and the animals that loved him so. One day, they all got together and wanted to do something special to show Farmer Jones how much they appreciated him.

They had a grand idea. They would make him the best breakfast ever. "I'll bring the eggs," cried the chicken. "And, I the milk," the cow chimed in. The pig thought about it long and hard. "Just how much do I love Farmer Jones?" he asked himself.

Knowing he loved him more than life itself, he spoke up. "I will bring the bacon," he said.

You see, the chicken and the cow, they were involved, but the pig, he was committed.

Progress, Not Perfection

If you are going to make it to the top of your game, it will take a bit of patience. Rome wasn't built in one day.

Athletes and artists work diligently just to qualify to compete. It takes more than just a pretty face or a perfectly limber body to get to where you're going. Ballet, contemporary dancing, gymnastics, cheerleading, it's all very hard work.

Here are a few suggestions you might heed along the way:

- Passion is everything. Love what you do… do what you love.
- Seek to learn from those you admire.
- Practice makes perfect.
- Eat healthy, get enough sleep, and drink plenty of water.
- Never quit.
- Pay as much attention to your mental conditioning as you do to your physical conditioning.
- Find balance both on the floor and in your personal life.
- Don't overload yourself.
- Be kind to yourself and others.
- Keep on your toes.
- Put your best foot forward.
- Stretch your limits, but never, ever limit your stretches.

Stretch your limits, but never, ever limit your stretches.

About the Author

CJ Jerabek is an accomplished and diversified author who writes on a wide variety of topics. She especially enjoys writing about subjects that are helpful to her readers such as health and fitness.

For this book, she teamed up with former professional ballet dancer and exercise instructor, Faye Viviana. Together, Jerabek and Viviana bring you the best of both worlds, expert stretching instructions from a pro and the creative writing that springs it all into action.

Readers can contact CJ by visiting www.14-peaks.com or emailing info@14-peaks.com

66567893R00065

Made in the USA
Lexington, KY
17 August 2017